before

The Life of
Clarence Birdseye

Tiffany Peterson

Heinemann
LIBRARY

www.heinemann/library.co.uk
Visit our website to find out more information about Heinemann Library books.

To order:
 Phone 44 (0) 1865 888066
Send a fax to 44 (0) 1865 314091
Visit the Heinemann Library Bookshop at www.heinemann/library.co.uk to browse our catalogue and order online.

First published in Great Britain by Heinemann Library,
Halley Court, Jordan Hill, Oxford OX2 8EJ,
part of Harcourt Education.
Heinemann is a registered trademark of Harcourt
Education Ltd.

Editorial: Angela McHaney Brown, Kathy Peltan
Design: Herman Adler Design
Map Illustrations: Yoshi Miyake
Picture Research: Carol Parden
Production: Edward Moore

Originated by QueNet™
Printed and bound by lake Book Manufacturing, Inc.,
USA

ISBN 0 431 18073 3
07 06 05 04 03
10 9 8 7 6 5 4 3 2 1

British Library Cataloguing in Publication Data

Peterson, Tiffany
   The Life of Clarence Birdseye
   338.7'66402853'092

A full catalogue record for this book is available from
the British Library.

Acknowledgements
The publishers would like to thank the following for
permission to reproduce photographs:
pp. 1, 5, 28 Brian Warling/Heinemann Library; p. 4 Japack
Company/Corbis; pp. 6, 9, 20, 22, 24 Brown Brothers; p. 7
Photodisc, Inc.; p. 8 Amherst College; pp. 11, 14, 15 The Peary-
MacMillan Arctic Museum/Bowdoin College; pp. 12, 13 North
Wind Picture Archives; p. 16 Galen Rowell/Corbis; pp.18, 25
Bettmann/Corbis; p. 21 Teich Company Collection/Lake County
Discovery Museum; pp. 23, 29 Agrilink Foods; p. 26 Pablo
Corral/Corbis; p. 27 Everett Collection

Cover photographs by Brian Warling/Heinemann Library and
Agrilink Foods

Special thanks to Michelle Rimsa for her comments in the
preparation of this book.

Contents

Any words in bold, **like this**, are explained in the Glossary

Frozen fresh foods

People need and want to eat vegetables all year.

Eating vegetables helps us stay healthy. There are many kinds of vegetables. Some, such as green beans, peas and sweet corn, become ripe in summer and autumn.

Clarence Birdseye found a way to freeze foods so they still taste fresh. With frozen foods, people can have vegetables, fruit and other foods at any time of year.

These frozen foods can be stored in a freezer for months.

Early years

Clarence Birdseye was born in 1886 in Brooklyn, New York in the USA. When he was a teenager, his family moved to Montclair, in the state of New Jersey.

This is how Brooklyn looked when Clarence lived there.

In Montclair, Clarence tried many new things. One thing he learned was the skill of **taxidermy**. In secondary school, he went to cooking lessons to learn new skills.

Clarence learned how to stuff animals. He could make them look almost like they did when they were alive.

College and work

In 1908, Clarence went to Amherst College in Massachusetts. He learned more about animals in his **biology** lessons. College cost a lot of money, though. Clarence needed money to pay for his studies.

One way young Clarence made money was by catching frogs. He sold them to the Bronx Zoo in New York City. They were fed to the snakes.

In 1910, Clarence ran out of money, so he left college. For a short time, he worked in an office in New York City. He also worked studying animals and the environment.

Clarence did many small jobs for people while he lived in New York. This is how the city looked at that time.

Fur trading

Clarence wanted to use what he had learned about animals in his job. So he decided to become a **fur trader**. In 1912, he went to Labrador, in Canada.

Clarence spent four years travelling around northern Canada selling furs.

Arctic Circle

Labrador Sea

Labrador

Labrador City

Newfoundland

Quebec

CANADA

N
W E
S

ATLANTIC OCEAN

Massachusetts

| 0 | 150 | 300 miles |
| 0 | 150 | 300 kilometres |

During the short, hot summers, Clarence travelled by boat to trade furs. In the long, cold winters, he travelled on a dogsled.

The easiest way for people to travel over the snow and ice in Labrador was by dogsled.

A family of his own

In 1915, Clarence went home to New Jersey for a visit. While he was there, he married Eleanor Gannett. He returned to Labrador, but Eleanor stayed behind. She was expecting the first of their four children.

In 1916, Clarence's wife and their new baby son joined Clarence in snowy Labrador.

Clarence worried about feeding his family during Labrador's long, cold winters.

Clarence wanted to be sure that his family always had enough to eat in Labrador. He needed to find a way to store food so it would not rot.

Frozen fish

One day, Clarence watched the local **Inuit** fishing. They pulled fish through a hole in the ice. As the fish came out of the cold, salty water, they quickly froze.

The fish that the Inuit caught and froze could be stored for months.

Clarence noticed something else. Once cooked, the fish that had been frozen tasted nearly as good as fresh fish.

Clarence learned from the Inuit how best to freeze different foods.

Testing it out

Clarence thought he could freeze other foods in the same way that the **Inuit** had frozen fish. He **experimented** with different foods. He froze cabbage and rabbit, duck and caribou meat.

Caribou are large deer that are found in Canada.

With frozen food supplies, Clarence's wife and son had plenty to eat.

Clarence followed the Inuit's example. First, he placed the food in cold, salty water. Then, he put it out in the wind. The food froze. And, it tasted fresh when it was cooked.

A new business

In 1917, the USA began fighting in World War I. Clarence decided he should move his family back to the USA.

When the USA went to war, Clarence's ideas about freezing food had to wait.

Clarence worked for three different companies during the war. After the war, he went back to **experimenting** with food. He wanted to find new ways to freeze it.

Clarence had to experiment using ice and an electric fan.

Quick-freezing

Clarence discovered a very good way to freeze food. He called it quick-freezing. Cold metal plates helped to freeze the food. They also pressed the food into small cardboard boxes.

Clarence created this machine to freeze and package foods.

People were used to eating fish fresh from the docks. Clarence knew frozen fish would have to taste just as fresh.

In 1924, Clarence found three people who were interested in his work with quick-freezing. Together, they started General Seafoods Company.

Success!

Clarence understood that people needed food packages that were easy to store in the freezer.

Clarence began selling his frozen foods in small cardboard packets. He sold frozen fish, meat, fruit and vegetables.

In 1929, General Foods bought Clarence's company. They renamed it 'Birds Eye Frosted Foods'. Clarence worked for the company. He kept **experimenting** and improving his process.

Birds Eye Frosted Foods were sold throughout the USA.

From freezing to drying

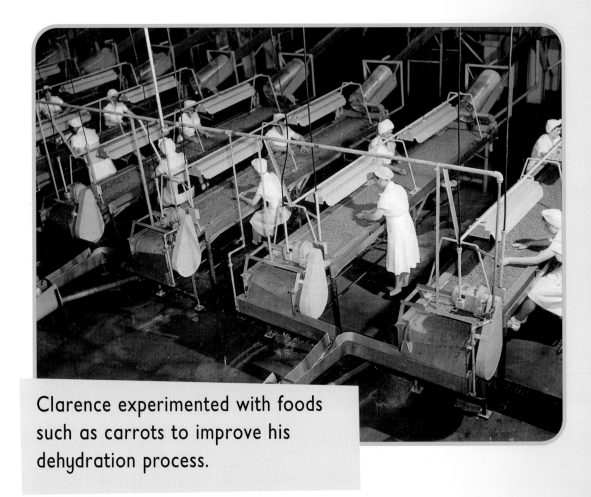

Clarence experimented with foods such as carrots to improve his dehydration process.

Clarence wanted to find other ways to store foods. He turned to drying foods, which is called **dehydration**. Dried foods can also be stored for months.

Clarence knew that freezing foods quickly **preserved** their fresh taste. He thought dehydrating quickly would have the same result. After six years of **experiments**, Clarence perfected his dehydration process.

Like his frozen foods, Clarence's dehydrated foods were packaged in small boxes.

A lifelong inventor

Clarence became a millionaire. He did not need to work any more. He enjoyed **experimenting**, though. So he kept working on new **inventions**.

Clarence invented many things, such as a heat lamp for keeping food warm.

Only Clarence or someone with his permission could make or sell his patented inventions.

On 7 October 1956, Clarence Birdseye died from heart trouble. By then, he had around 300 **patents**.

Learning more about Clarence Birdseye

Birds Eye still packages frozen foods in small, easy-to-store cardboard boxes or plastic bags.

Clarence Birdseye was not the first person to freeze foods. But his quick-freezing method continues to be the best way to **preserve** fresh flavours.

Today, the company Clarence started is called Birds Eye Foods. The company still works hard to give people fresh-tasting frozen foods.

Today, Clarence Birdseye's name is known around the world.

Fact file

- Clarence Birdseye is known as the 'Father of Quick-freezing'.
- He liked to play Chinese chequers and to give large dinner parties.
- Clarence always liked **experimenting** with plants.
  While he was in Peru, he found a way to make paper out of **sugar-cane** stalks.
- Clarence and his wife, Eleanor, worked together to write a book called *Growing Woodland Plants*.
- The Birdseyes had four children, two boys and two girls.

Timeline

9 December 1886	Clarence Birdseye is born
1912	Clarence becomes a **fur trader** in Labrador, Canada
1915	Clarence marries Eleanor Gannett, after writing letters to her for years
1917	Clarence moves his family back to the USA
1924	Clarence forms the General Seafoods Company
1925	The company starts selling quick-frozen meat
1929	Birds Eye Frosted Foods company is formed
1932	First Birds Eye vegetables are sold in shops
7 October 1956	Clarence dies from heart trouble

Glossary

biology study of living things, such as plants and animals

dehydration drying out food so it can be stored longer

experiment test that is done to discover or prove something

fur trader person who buys and sells animal furs

Inuit native person of the North American Arctic, also known as Eskimo

invention new thing or new idea of how to do something

patent legal paper given to a person that says he or she is the only person allowed to make a certain invention unless special permission is given

preserve keep the same

sugar-cane tall plant that is used to make sugar

taxidermy process of preparing, stuffing and mounting dead animals to make them look like they did when they were alive

More books to read

Food: Peas, Louise Spilsbury, (Heinemann Library, 2002)

Look After Yourself: Healthy Food, Angela Royston, (Heinemann Library, 2003)

Safe and Sound: Eat Well, Angela Royston, (Heinemann Library, 2000)

Index